ISBN 978-1-333-76916-1
PIBN 10545630

1 MONTH OF
FREE
READING

at

www.ForgottenBooks.com

By purchasing this book you are eligible for one month membership to ForgottenBooks.com, giving you unlimited access to our entire collection of over 700,000 titles via our web site and mobile apps.

To claim your free month visit:
www.forgottenbooks.com/free545630

YOU MUST LABOR FOR SALVATION.

BY REV. DAVID SHAVER, RICHMOND, VA.

Human life is a pilgrimage. We are all travellers to eternity. Not one of us but must depart from this world, and go out into a world to come. Every day and every night bears us onward—still ouward—hence—thither! But all are not passing over the same road; all are not journeying to the same place. There is a broad thoroughfare to hell, and the overwhelming majority of men throng that. Only a small minority—one here, and there another—toils along the narrow ascent to heaven. This is not the teaching of presumptuous ignorance on the part of the enthusiast, or of austere rigor on the part of the bigot. Our Saviour himself declares it: "Wide is the gate and broad is the way that leadeth to destruction, and many there be which go in thereat: Because strait is the gate and narrow is the way which leadeth unto life, and few there be which find it." (Matt. 7; 13, 14.)

The most important of all questions, therefore, for every one of us, is, How may we join ourselves to "the little flock" that finds and follows the way of life? It is the obvious dictate of reason, that we must form earnest purposes and make strenuous efforts to gain the path that leads to the peace and the presence of God; that multitudes fail in this endeavor because their purposes are inconstant or their efforts inefficient; that mere *seeking* will not suffice here—there must be *striving*. But we have not been left to gather this truth from uncertain reasonings of our own. It, also, has come to us from the lips of our Saviour: "Strive to enter in at the strait gate; for many, I say unto you, will seek to enter in, and shall not be able." (Luke 13; 24.)

In these passages of Scripture, then, we have the plain but most momentous doctrine, that *those who wish to secure the salvation of the soul must be earnest, resolute, laborious.* Will you suffer your thoughts to dwell on it?

I. Those who wish to secure the salvation of the soul! And who are they? Perhaps all who read these lines who are yet out of Christ. Few, indeed, are the persons who grow so callous and reprobate, so insane in spiritual things, as deliberately and utterly to renounce all desire of eternal life.

A Christian minister, once, during the progress of a revival, went to an unconverted man who sat indifferent in the congregation, and asked, "My friend—do you not wish to go to heaven when you die?" That unconverted man, who was not so much as lifting his little finger to reach the kingdom of glory, who gave not the slightest heed to the truth, who evinced not a shadow of feeling under the out-pouring of the Spirit—that unconverted man replied, "Sir, do you think I am a fool?" and left the house, indignant that he should be accounted so stupid and so blind as not to wish for a home in heaven, when earth could provide him a home no longer.

We do not think that our impenitent readers are fools, in the sense of this question and reply. No: not one of them. With some vague and fluctuating, half-nursed, half-smothered feeling, they wish to secure the salvation of their souls—they know not *how*—they decide not *when*. Now, be it borne in mind by them, that this wish will serve·no good purpose—will deceive, betray, destroy them, if they are not earnest, resolute, laborious about the matter. All Scripture says so. "Ye shall seek me and find me, when ye shall search for me *with all your heart*." (Jer. 29 ; 13.) "Blessed are they which *do hunger and thirst after* righteousness : for they shall be filled." (Matt. 5 ; 6.) "Let us *labor*, therefore, to enter into that rest, lest any man fall after the same example of unbelief." (Heb. 4 ; 11.) " *Work out* your own salvation *with fear and trembling ;* for it is God that worketh in you to will and to do of his good pleasure." (Phil. 2 ; 13.) These passages, with a thousand others, utter in our ears the warning—"all our heart, and all our soul, and all our mind, and all our strength," must be concentrated on the great work of salvation.

This doctrine, we know, is an unwelcome one. Man loves to have salvation made easy. With as little trouble and as little toil as possible would he obtain God's favor and clothe himself with Christ's righteousness. His ear is reluctant to hear, his heart to heed, the voice which cries, "Give diligence to make your calling and election· sure." The decision and energy, the bending of the inner man with all its might, the waking and the working and the warring, necessary to a genuine Christian experience, are pared down, and frittered away, until men hope to be " carried to the skies on flowery beds of ease."

Who can doubt this, when he hears a Roman Catholic bishop say, that his "church would not desire more than two hours to prepare any man for death?"

Who can doubt it, when·he learns that a distinguished

Protestant divine preached a sermon, to prove that it requires no more time to fit a man for heaven, 'than is necessary for these two propositions to pass through his mind,—I have sinned,—Christ died for sinners?

Oh, most fatal delusion, persuading our natural slothfulness in spiritual matters, that we can enter in at the strait gate without *striving*, without even *seeking*, in any reasonable sense of the terms! And it is in this way that man would fain enter. This is the rock on which thousands, who hope to gain the eternal haven, split and go down in the waters of an overwhelming wrath. Dear reader take better counsel. Only the earnest, resolute, laborious, have a guarantee of salvation; only those who search for the Lord with all their heart—who hunger and thirst after righteousness—who labor to enter into that rest—who work out their own salvation with fear and trembling. In all the word of God, from first to last, there is not one syllable of promise to any other soul of man. No ray of hope shines out from the inspired pages but for the *striver* alone. Even the *seeker*, inconstant, inefficient, fails, and for him no place is prepared in the bosom of divine love.

II. What we have said will suffice. with the thoughtful reader, to show the importance of this doctrine. We pass now to enquire, Why is it necessary that we be earnest, resolute, laborious, to secure the salvation of the soul? Why is it that we cannot enter the Strait Gate, except we *strive* to effect an entrance?

(1.) It is not because man is required to be his own saviour, and, by a wisdom and a strength which are his, to accomplish the work that makes him a child and an heir of God. Far otherwise. "He that sitteth in the heavens" instructs us to style *Him* " our Saviour." (Tit. 3; 4.) " According to His mercy, *He* saves us." (Tit. 3; 5.)

On His head alone must the crown of salvation be put. He will suffer His creatures to wear it, no, not for a moment.

But it is because man wishes to take this crown from God's head, and place it upon his own. Because by nature we are ambitious to save ourselves; to give the credit of our salvation to our strength and our wisdom. Because it requires a sore struggle to suddue this proud disposition, which has many lives, which comes forth often from the grave we put it in as dead, and needs to be often slain. Because none but an earnest spirit will hew down this tree of carnal independence, and pluck it up, and cast it utterly into the fire, sparing not one fibre of its roots—not even one twig of its branches. Because it is a hard and difficult thing for self-exalting man sincerely to say, "Not unto us, O Lord, not unto us, but unto thy name give glory." (Psa. 115; 1.)

(2.) It is not because God entertains a personal, acrimonious hostility towards sinners, and is inclined to withhold salvation from them, and stands aloof until something be done to inspire Him with a disposition to accept them. Indeed it is not. "I have no pleasure in the death of him that dieth, saith the Lord." (Ez. 18; 32.) "God is in Christ reconciling the world unto Himself, not imputing their trespasses unto them." (2 Cor. 5; 19.) "The Lord is long-suffering to usward, not willing that any should perish, but that all should come to repentance." (2 Pet. 3; 9.)

But it is because unbelief, reigning in the heart, denies or distrusts the readiness of God to accept us in the Beloved. Because unbelief credits the father of lies, when he slanderously represents the Most High as a cruel tyrant, reluctant to pardon the rebellious. Because unbelief persuades us that there is a sternness and enmity in the bosom of the Lord, which calls for softening on our behalf. Because unbelief fosters the impression that tears, distresses, agonies, are demanded in order to move our Father in heaven to a pity which He does not feel without them. Because man clings to this unbelief; and will not break through its barriers to a Saviour's open arms; and puts his hand into its hand to be led away from the cross; and refuses to tear aside the veil it throws over his eyes, and see how swift our offended Judge is to run to meet the returning prodigal while yet a great way off.

(3.) It is not because the salvation which is God's gift—a gift bestowed with utmost willingness—nevertheless requires some fitness on our part to go before it; some previous good works to make us worthy of it; some excellencies of character and life to purchase or at least procure it. By no means. "Not by works of righteousness which we have done, but according to His mercy He saved us, by the washing of regeneration and renewing of the Holy Ghost." (Tit. 3; 5.) "By deeds of the law there shall no flesh be justified in His sight. But to him who worketh not"—that is, to merit justification by deeds of the law—to him who in this sense worketh not, "but believeth on Him who justifieth the ungodly, his faith is counted for righteousness." (Ro. 3; 20, 4; 5.)

But it is because God who saves us, does not save us without ourselves. Because He does not make us His, as He might raise up children to Abraham out of stones, with no consent or co-operation of our own. Because, when He works in us, He works, not to dispense with our willing and our doing, but works that we ourselves may will, that we ourselves may do. Because He lays hold of all the powers of our nature which have been active to perform evil in His sight, and demands that these very powers, every one of them, should with equal activity employ themselves to seek Him and to serve Him, without accounting it meritorious in them to do so; without forgetting that enough of imperfection mars this labor, enough of sin defiles it, to show that even by it the law is broken—that a washing in Christ's blood is indispensable even for it.

Take now the truth, partly implied, partly · expressed, in these last remarks. In saving us, God brings into exercise our liberty of will and our capacity for action. He finds us asleep, and does not lift us in His arms and carry us, still sleeping, within the gate of life. But He arouses us from our slumber, and calls us to arise, and moves us to walk and to run along the right way until *we* enter into that gate. Now, in thus laboring for our salvation, what are the hindrances which we must surmount? Are these hindrances so great that only an earnest, resolute, laborious spirit will force a passage through? Let us see.

(1.) There is an evil nature which must be changed. Sin reigns not only over the life, but in the soul. The heart, the very heart itself, is wrong; like the waters of Marah, bitter and unwholesome—needing that the tree of life should be cast into the waters to make them sweet. Appetence, affection, passion, must be renewed; must have the tendrils which creep along the earth, and fasten themselves to it, unloosed and raised aloft, and entwined around the things of God, that they may grow upward. God's power, indeed, effects this transformation of nature: but we must be willing, anxious—freely choosing it, earnestly desiring it, diligently seeking it. Can we, with facility, bring ourselves to this frame of mind? Oh, hard, hard task for the proud human heart! "It is easier to set a man against all the world than against himself; and yet a man must be set against himself, in order to his conversion."

(2.) There are evil habits which must be broken off.

Every wrong feeling of our nature inclines us to do evil in the sight of God; to repeat to-day the evil we did yesterday—and to-morrow the evil we are doing to-day. Ah; the waters are not only bitter; they are flowing—flowing downward—widening their channels—becoming more and yet more rapid in their descent. Now, if we would save our souls, against this deepening and accelerating current must we swim: the current itself must be turned back; old habits destroyed,—new and better habits formed. The way of wickedness familiar to our feet must be forsaken; and over no part of that long-trodden path must they be allowed to wander again. What we have been accustomed to do, must be done no longer. What we have been accustomed to omit, must be omitted no longer. But, habit—strong habit—mighty habit—we had almost said omnipotent habit,—who does not know that the utmost force of character barely suffices to overcome it? Who does not know that for its conquest, the mind's steadiest, staunchest, stablest inflexibility must come into operation?

(3.) There are evil maxims, or rules of conduct, which must be renounced. If repentance and faith have their codes, so also have unbelief and impenitence. These strive to be a law unto themselves. How many are the false principles which they set up here and there along our course through life, as way-marks to guide the feet, but wofully misguiding them! At times, sinners think that religion suits well the old, but that young persons should see and enjoy much of the world before they renounce worldly pleasure. At times they think that they must lie supine in spiritual matters, like lifeless clods, until a mighty down-coming of grace irresistibly sweeps them into the kingdom of heaven. At times, they think that a more convenient season is prepared for them, somewhere in the future, when no difficulties shall defeat or dispute their return to the Lord. At times, they think that mere moral reformation, and cold and formal devotions, will put them into the Saviour's bosom, and fold His arms about them lovingly and tenderly. But who can number all the forms which sin's excuses for its sinfulness may wear? Who shall say into how many refuges of lies the heart of unbelief runs, to hide itself from the searching light of truth. "Their name is legion." They are plausible, too—plausible in the eyes of the evil nature to which they appeal—plausible through the power of the evil habits with which they accord. A deceived heart loves them well; and catches the hand that would pluck their mask away; and will not let their hollowness stand exposed ; and, if the mask be, now and then, disturbed, carefully adjusts it again, that the deception may 'go bravely on.' How hardly, then, shall the bosom be purged of their leaven!

(4.) There are evil examples which must be resisted. The allusion is not simply to habits of gross vice. All examples are evil which involve *delayed* repentance and faith *postponed;* all are evil which encourage ' this post-ponement of faith, this delay of repentance. Evil, because if the soul treads in their steps, they shall lead it down to the pit; because they have led it almost thither at this present. And such examples are around. us everywhere. They are in the community—in scenes of business—in places of amusement—in the circle of friendship—in the household. They are associated with the dignity of age and the charm of youth ; with beauty's smile and talent's spell ; with wealth, and influence, and official station; with education, morality, refinement, high regard, deep love. They speak the same language, they impel to the same course, with the evil nature we inherit—and the evil habits we indulge—and the evil maxims we embrace. Surely, then, if we bestir not ourselves, they will carry us away as with a flood—as the tempestuous gale sweeps the unresisting bird along its track.

Such are the hindrances which oppose our entrance into the Strait Gate. Evil nature! Evil habits! Evil maxims! Evil examples! Four strong and massive chains, riveted upon our enslaved souls. How strenuous must the *striving* be which would break loose! How absolutely without hope is the sinner, who attempts the work of salvation in any other than an earnest, resolute, laborious spirit! Oh, it is for the want of this spirit that thousands who are brought nigh to the kingdom of God, go away backward, and never set foot in it. Halyburton, in the course of three years, ascertained that out of four hundred persons in his congregation, there were only about forty who would not confess, that, at some time or other, they had been more or less awakened by the word. And why did these three hundred and sixty persons relapse into carnal slumber again? Why were their convictions quenched, their souls unsaved? They lacked an earnest, resolute, laborious spirit. They did not strive to enter in at the Strait Gate. Yes: *not striving is the way to death and hell.* Turn from it we entreat you, dear reader, on the instant.

III. We cannot refrain from affectionately urging you just here, to stand on your guard against the great temptation which Satan will seek to draw from this doctrine. If he can, he will incline you to say that as it is so difficult to work out your own salvation now, you will put off the hard and irksome task. Oh, hear him not. Delay can only aggravate the difficulties of the case. *An evil nature* will reign in your bosom with but a more tyrannous and irresistible sway, because that sway has been longer confirmed. *Evil habits* will wax stronger and stronger through indulgence. It has been said that "habits are like crocodiles; as long as they live, they grow." You will find the saying true. And you will find how true is that other saying : "an evil habit is a hook in the soul, and draws it whithersoever the devil pleases." *Evil maxims*, too, will more thoroughly imbue the mind ; and diffuse their leaven through all processes of thought; and take, increasingly, the color of undisputed truths ; and stand like unremovable guide-posts along the way of your life. *Evil Examples*, also, as friendship deepens in degree or widens in its circle, as you have the oftener seen with the eyes, or trodden in the steps, or yielded to the persuasion of others,—evil examples will be mightier things with you. All these elements of difficulty in the work of salvation, then, gather power from delay. Of these chains around the soul, the links grow more massive—the rivets are fastened more securely. And then, the Spirit of grace may abandon you! And then, again, life may be suddenly cut short! Oh, there is desert of damnation, there may be damnation, in the purpose not to strive *now* to enter in at the Strait Gate. If you form that purpose, remember Christ's words : "Many shall seek to enter in, *and shall not be able.*" Beware lest you yourselves stand outcast and condemned among that number. Beware : to-day is given for striving; to-morrow, the punishment of not striving may fall as an avalanche of terror and wrath upon you. Beware : " God comes with leaden feet, but strikes with iron hands"—comes tardily and noiselessly—strikes terribly and crushingly. Beware : "the mill of God grinds late, but grinds to powder!" Beware : the voice which speaks from heaven says, "Their foot shall slide in due time; for the day of their calamity is at hand ; and the things that shall come upon them make haste." (Deut. 32; 35.)

IV. And now, it remains to ask, When the sinner, shrinking from such a doom, is aroused to an earnest, resolute, laborious spirit in the matter of salvation, how will that spirit manifest itself? What will the striver do, to effect an entrance into the Strait Gate?

(1.) An earnest, resolute, laborious spirit in the matter of salvation will lead to *frequent and persevering private devotion.* He whose eyes are opened to spiritual things, and whose feelings are rightly wrought upon by them, will find out some place of retirement. He will get himself apart from man, to commune in solitude with the God whom he seeks.—*Prayer* will be his work there. He will cry to the Strong for strength. He will pour his fears and hopes, his perplexities and desires, his confessions of sin and supplications for pardon, into the ears of the Lord, struggling against unbelief, entreating the gift of faith.— *The Bible* will be his companion there. He will consult its pages for guidance in the way of life. He will hear Christ speaking in it. He will search it for the answer to the question, " What must I do to be saved ? " He will lay up its teachings in his heart, that they may bring him *straight* to the cross.

(2.) That spirit will lead to *regular attendance on the public means of grace.* The Lord's day will not dawn unwelcomely to the awakened and enquiring sinner. He will be prompt and punctual in going up to the courts of the Lord's house. And he will have for the exercises of the Lord's worship a patient and respectful heed. As often as opportunity allows, he will wait on the ministration of the word, if peradventure there may be in it a special message from the Lord to him. His will not be a vacant seat at church; because to occupy it would subject him to inconvenience. Unless necessity constrains him, he will not be simply " a Sunday morning hearer," as too many who call themselves Christians are. He will arrange his business so as to find time for appearing in the sanctuary, or, if this cannot be done, he will neglect his business that

his soul may be saved. He will do these things, because
the great majority of those now in glory have been met by
the Lord in the congregations of His people. Zion has
been *their* birth-place; he will hasten thither if haply there
he too may be born from above, of the Spirit. He will
often come, lest when one spark of truth has been struck
into his bosom, it should be extinguished before another,
and another, and another have been added to it to kindle
a flame; lest when the means of grace have borne him one
step upward, worldly influences should beat him back again,
before these means have opportunity to bear him, step by
step, on, still on, toward heaven.

(3.) That spirit will lead to *religious conference with Christians.* The striver after God's grace, conscious of his own
ignorance, will desire instruction from those who have been
made partakers of that grace. Once, shame sealed his
lips, and he was far from all willingness to unbosom himself to believers. But now, wishing for their sympathy,
he struggles against this snare of the devil, and asks those
who walk the path of life to reach forth a helping hand
and aid his approaches to Christ. He will permit warning and counsel from men of God; he will seek it. Or, if
he shrinks from conversation, face to face, he will call his
pen into use, and put his case on paper, and submit his
doubtings, his enquirings, his yearnings, to such as he
deems able to bring the truth out, in its application to
himself. He will not forget nor dishonor the will of God,
to teach those who would be His people by means of those
who are.

(4.) That spirit will lead to *abstinence from worldly
scenes and pleasures.* He in whom this spirit dwells will
shun the things that are calculated to impair and expel it.
He will turn away from the places where thoughtlessness,
mirth and vanity reign, and catch like running flame from

heart to heart, and scorch and wither the tender germs of penitence. Songs, dances and revellings are not iu unison with his frame of mind then; they pall on his taste in mere anticipation, and he stands aloof from them. Alas for him, if by the persuasion of others, or his own unsteadfastness, this reluctance is overcome. Alas,—it may cost him his soul! A sense of God's wrath had fallen on Luther Rice—a sense, too, of his own sinfulness. A lady, who knew not the way of life, advised him to avoid these gloomy views of his character and condition, and for this purpose, to mingle in gay society and share its gayeties. Did not her counsel proceed on this principle—that worldly amusements are fitted to erase serious impressions from the mind? And are not amusements adapted to so fearful an office? Have not thousands sought them with no other aim? and succeeded to put out the kindlings of repentance within them? and made the heart that was softening, hard again—harder than ever before? and gone away from the Saviour joyfully—to find him never after—never in time or in eternity? Oh, it cannot be doubted: thev are expedients of Satan for quenching the Spirit in human bosoms—potent expedients. And as such, the sinner, truly alive to his guilt and his danger, *will* fly from them; *must*, if he be not resolved to throw his soul away.

(5) That spirit will lead to *an open espousal of Christ's cause.* Genuine and absorbing desire for eternal life will make no secret of itself. The work of repentance and faith will not be done in a corner. Confession of sin will be as open as sin itself; standing on God's side, as public as standing among aliens and enemies to Him. He is but partially awakened who strives to put his light of truth, as it were, into a dark lantern, that no eye but his own may see it; that it may shine secretly for him, and no one else discern it. In such a lantern that light will not shine

even for him; it will go out, soon or later, in utter midnight.

Are you willing, dear reader, to engage in this work—the work for which man's life was given—the work which draws after it eternal life? Are you resolved to begin *at once* the warfare against an evil nature, evil habits, evil maxims, evil examples? Then, "be of good courage." You have the word of God to teach you. You have the blood of Christ to cleanse you. · You have the Spirit of holiness to guide and strengthen you. Strive hopefully, therefore, *relying on these, for the grace of striving.* Strive to get to the cross, as a penitent for sin and a believer in free justification from sin. Strive to ascend from the cross along the pathway of childlike obedience, to the kingdom and crown of righteousness. And may *the Saviour of the striver* grant you that "salvation which is in Him, with eternal glory!"

S. M.

'Tis God the Spirit leads
　In paths before unknown:
The work to be performed is ours,
　The strength is all His own.

Supported by His grace,
　We still pursue our way,
And hope at last to reach the prize,
　Secure in endless day.

'Tis He that works to will,
　'Tis He that works to do ;
The power by which we act is His,
　And His the glory too.

L. M.

My gracious Lord, I own thy right
   To every service I can pay,
And call it my supreme delight
   To hear thy dictates and obey.

What is my being but for thee—
   Its sure support, its noblest end ?
'Tis my delight thy face to see,
   And serve the cause of such a Friend.

I would not sigh for worldly joy,
   Or to increase my worldly good :
Nor future days nor powers employ
   To spread a sounding name abroad.

'Tis to my Saviour I would live—
   To Him who for my ransom died ;
Nor could all worldly honor give
   Such bliss as crowns me at His side.

His work my hoary age shall bless,
   When youthful vigor is no more,
And my last hour of life confess
   His saving love, His glorious power.

CPSIA information can be obtained
at www.ICGtesting.com
Printed in the USA
LVHW021322071118
596294LV00005B/862

9 781333 769161